SECOND THOUGHTS

A book of Poems

by Pat McCann

Copyright © 2017 by Pat McCann

All rights reserved. This book or any portion thereof may not be reproduced or used in any manner whatsoever without the express written permission of the publisher except for the use of brief quotations in a book review or scholarly journal.

First Printing :2017

ISBN 978-1-326-96508-2

Pat McCann

Dublin

Ireland

Introduction

Having already published my first book of poetry and shared some of my work on the internet, I feel it is time to test the waters again with a follow on to
"Thoughts at Arms Length";
Welcome to my new book of poems which is titled
"Second Thoughts".

While making preparations for this book I take the opportunity to acknowledge and thank all of those close and dear friends who assisted with both the editing and sales of the first book. Particularly to Pat O'Hanlon who introduced the book to her many friends in her wide social circle.

Also to Bobby O'Grady (Bobby's Rambles) for his article in *"Three Rock Panorama"* and not forgetting Minister Shane Ross TD (*Minister for Transport, Tourism and Sport),* who wrote the foreword for it.

Finally, a big 'thank you' to all those who read and commented on my first venture into the world of poetic verse.

~~~~~~

Index

1. Peace in my Valley
2. Out of step
3. Monty the Dancing Mouse
4. Eyes
5. Remembrance
6. Legato
7. Evening glow
8. Saturday Afternoon (Dublin '63)
10. Beespoke
11. Morning Epiphany
12. Echoes
13. Achill
14. Who?
16. Cherry Blossoms
17. Awakening
18. Down all Our Yesterdays
19. Homer's Sillylad
20. The Lamb
21. Restoring
22. The Hour glass

23 Rhapsody
24 By the Lake
25 Dreamer
26 Into the Stillness
27 Tomorrows Task Today
28 Maude and Claude
29 Lament
30 The Source
32 Starscape
33 Tidal Urge
34 Life's Threshold
35 Ode to a Duck
36 Faded Dreams
38 Orchestration
39 Placid Waters
40 Repose
41 Orpheus
42 Mistified
43 The Masters Voice
44 Golden Epilogue

Peace in my Valley.

The fragrance of the heathers scent,
Drifts across the wooded dell.
Shadows cast by a silver moon
Create a mystical spell.
The peace and stillness of the night
Becalms the cares of day
And whispers from a flowing stream
Soothes apprehension away.
The quiet of this outer world
Slowly transfers to within,
In harmony with the spirit
Relaxation can begin.
How restful then my valley feels,
Peace and comfort to restore.
Where the heart, the mind and nature
Intertwine in sweet rapport.

****

Out of Step

I of the world and in the world,
Have marched in step, in time.
The world it played its melody,
Exquisite and sublime.
Never a stumble in the stride
Along the worldly way.
I grasped at every chance I passed,
But who was left to pay?

I of the world and in the world
Now full of introspection.
From left to right or right to left,
Unsure of my direction.
No more the footfall keeping pace
To the cadence of the tune.
My flag has reached its time to furl,
In life's late afternoon.

****

Monty the Dancing Mouse

A recent visitor to our house
After four long days of rain.
A funny little cheeky mouse,
That entered through the drain.
He playfully would squeal and prance
Across our kitchen floor.
With forward flips or sideway slips
And a Salsa his encore.
His acrobatics made us laugh,
The kids would shout with glee;
As Monty Mouse would waltz to Strauss
A one and two and three.
He'd entertain us every day,
There's no mistaking that.
But it's been quiet since he danced…
The Rhumba with the cat.

~~~~~~~~~~~~~~~~~~~~~~~~~~~

EYES

Forever in my memory,
A rapture so divine.
As those eyes of love so tender,
Engaged longingly with mine.

Heart melting with the recall,
Of that first glance so sublime.
A window opened to our souls,
When our eyes did first combine.

A faded picture takes me back,
Though years have passed away.
Those haunting eyes, so filled with love
Smile back at me today.

~~~~~~~~~~~~~~~~~~~~~~~~~~~

REMEMBRANCE

Sometimes my mind will wander,
Recalling days gone by.
To patriotic heroes,
That time cannot deny.

Of those that sacrificed their lives,
So others might be free.
Who stood at conflicts bulwark;
In the name of liberty.

Their names now carved forever
in the annals of the brave.
For flag, for faith, for freedom,
Their lives they freely gave.

We elevate these martyrs,
Who sacrificed their all.
To snap the rod of serfdom,
In reply to country's call.

~~~~~~~~~~~~~~~~~~~~~~~~~~~~

Legato

The lightest strain of music,
Upon my ear descends.
As placid as the deepest lake,
The senses it transcends.
Melodic in its sequence,
So soothing in its vein.
Soft, serene and smooth as silk,
with peaceful, calm refrain.
A ripple of tranquility,
Through light orchestral sound.
Melody and harmony,
Within its structure found.
Tchaikovsky or Stravinsky,
Strauss or Massenet.
Music's charms enrapture,
To ease your cares away.

****

Evening Glow

As the golden orb sinks slowly
And the evening has begun.
A song thrush on an old oak branch,
Sings its praise to setting sun.
Deeply golden glows the evening
'neath the fading skies of blue.
Dusky shades of night approaching
Adding purple to the hue.
Gently now this Autumn gloaming,
Yields its charm to dwindling light.
Faintly twinkling stars appearing,
Nature's watchmen of the night.

++++++++++++++++++++++++++++

Saturday Afternoon (Dublin '63)

My Daydreams sometimes take me
Away into the past.
When life it had a gentle pace
And didn't move so fast.

This reverie to me recalls
Just how it used to be;
On Saturdays in Dublin town
In nineteen sixty three.

We'd get the bus in to the pillar
Where Nelson nobly stood.
Then into the Rainbow Café,
Where the ice cream was so good.

You could have a Melancholy Baby
that cost just one and three;
Or a knickerbocker glory
Before ya' had yer' tea.

Our next stop it was Woolworths,
The store that had it all.
Across the road from Moore Street,
With street traders wall to wall.

Then we'd go up Nelsons pillar,
Sure it was the thing to do.
We'd stay up there for ages
Just takin' in the view.

The day it wouldn't be the same
If we didn't check the style.
So up the street to Burtons,
We'd ramble for a while.

We tried on Crombie overcoats
and blazers just for fun.
By then the time was knockin' on,
For our bus we'd have to run.

Back home then to the Ma's and Da's,
With coddle for yer dinner.
Those memories of Saturdays,
will always be a winner.

~~~~~~~~~~~~~~~~~~~~~~~~~~~

Beespoke

You've been a busy bee, my dear,
Oh such a busy bee.
A busier bee than me, my dear,
Much busier than me.

You tend to flit and play, my love,
Though not so much with me.
Your life is such a rush my love,
As you dart from tree to tree.

Your nectar gathering, my sweet,
So marvellous to see.
The buzz you generate, my sweet,
Of a perfect honey bee.

The hive is filling up, my pet,
With nectar wall to wall.
It's sticking to my wings, my pet,
Now I can't fly at all.

'Twas not a clever choice, my dear,
To gather on this scale.
From head to toe I'm stuck, my dear
And the sting is in the tale.

****

Morning Epiphany

Mid the early morning chorus
An epiphany to dawn.
Nature's lyrical reflection,
In the glory of the morn.
Borne upon the call of songbird,
Softly falling on the ear.
Bidding welcome to the sunrise,
With a cadence crystal clear.
Slowly now the world is waking,
No longer darkness holding sway,
Aureate shafts of rising sunlight
Herald in another day.

~~~~~~~~~~~~~~~~~~~~~~~

ECHOES

Whispering echoes in my mind.
Memories flooding, free and fast.
Tunes of yesteryear I find,
Resonate from days - now past.

Foghorns lonely blast at sea,
Or the sound of distant bell,
Awake a haunting reverie
That bodes of sad farewell.

Yet echoes of a lilting strain,
Can enthral an empty heart.
With rousing verse or sweet refrain,
Grief and sadness soon depart.

Times echoed in my reminisce,
Seeing both sides of the moon
And lived again in dread or bliss
Through life's late afternoon.

~~~~~~~~~~~~~~~~~~~~~~~~~

Lovely Achill

Achill my lovely Achill,
Isle of the western sea
Achill my lovely Achill,
The place where I'm longing to be.

In search of fame and of fortune,
I ventured over the foam.
But Achill my lovely Achill,
Now you are calling me home.

Once again I will stroll by your ocean side
Golden beaches and rugged seashore
Hear the wash of the waves,
Thru the rocks and the caves
With an echo that lasts evermore

Achill my lovely Achill,
I'll walk on your green hills again
Achill my lovely Achill,
To the peaks then back down to the glen.

See the Moon rising over your hilltops
And the Sun setting down in the sea
Achill my lovely Achill,
Forever my home you will be.

WHO?

Who switches on the stars at night,
When the Sun has gone to rest?
Who was it taught the birds to fly
And how to build a nest?

Who is it causes wind to blow
And whistle through the trees?
Or how to make a honeycomb,
Who showed that to the bees?

Where do roses get their scent
When they're in fullest bloom?
Who is it paints the colours on
The peacocks feathered plume?

Who tells the tide when to go out,
Then when it shall return?
And to make a perfect cobweb,
How did the spider learn?

How do salmon find their way
To the spot where they were born?
After crossing Seas and Oceans,
In that same spot they will spawn

Who trains the blackbird how to sing
And the parrot how to speak?
Who makes each little snowflake
So different and unique?

These wondrous joys are gifted
To man from God above
All part of His creation
And His everlasting love

****

Cherry Blossom

Pastel and pink the petals float,
From the tree down to the ground.
Clothing the lawn as in a gown,
Without the slightest sound.

Breezes that whisper through the leaves,
Soothing as a maiden's sigh.
A restful, rhythmic, rhapsody,
Natures' springtime lullaby.

Oh Sweetest, scented, cherry pink.
Flower fragile, fine and fair.
Your fragrance fills the senses,
In the April evening air.

The blackbird sings its song of love,
With a cadence, sweet and free,
Celebrating the creation,
Of the cherry blossom tree.

~~~~~~~~~~~~~~~~~~~~~~~~~~~~~

Awakening

O' Darkness of winter
Cast off your cloak..
Leave your saddening gloom
With the Ides of March.
Allow the greening land be illumed;
As gushing streams sing.

Let May keep the promises of April rain,
Producing an ecstatic beauty of new growth.
Gently, the Sun shall warm the buds awake,
While delicate birdsong fills the air
And we with Mother Nature
Will dance to their tune.

~~~~~~~~~~~~~~~~~~~~~~~~~~~~~~~~~~

Down All our yesterdays

Behind you there are heartaches,
Behind you also joy.
Behind you are the crumbling ruins
That were meant to reach the sky.

Behind you there is new life
Still seeking out its way.
Behind you there are rainbows
That promised a new day.

Behind you love and laughter,
Behind you tears and pain.
Behind you is that special friend
To pick you up again.

Behind you there are victories,
Behind you there is loss.
Behind you lies an inner strength
That helps to bear each cross.

Behind you there is family,
Behind you there are friends.
Behind you there is God on high
Your problems He transcends.

****

HOMERS SILLYLAD

In days of yore, in Greek folklore,
You may have read of Spartacus.
But none so rare, who could compare,
With Homers Silly lad Barticus.
From the age of ten he stood with the men
And battled with foes that were tough.
With sword and with spear, he never would fear,
As he drank from a can labelled **'Duff'**.
This lad's dad Homer, was never a roamer,
At home all the day he would stay.
Living in modesty, writing an odyssey,
While his wife Margeretus turned grey.
In the depth of night, before the fight,
Barticus felt no remorse.
With a couple of swigs of Red Bull with figs,
He hid in the Trojan Horse.
As high as the sky, now the battle was nigh,
He jumped to the ground with a roar
And came face to face with a woman of grace,
Her like he had ne'er seen before.
She had hips that launched a thousand ships,
Together life they would enjoy.
In the throes of romance they began Zorba's Dance,
Homer's Silly lad and Helen of Troy.

****

THE LAMB

On a cold and still night on a hillside alone
Sat a shepherd there minding his sheep.
With frost in the air he was chilled to the bone,
He longed both for warmth and for sleep.

Then the stillness was broken with glorious sound
Of Angelic choirs singing on high.
"Glory, Glory." Rang out their song all around,
While a bright star lit up the night sky.

The star settled over an old cattle stall
Just down in the valley below.
An animal shelter so tiny and small
Lit up by that star all aglow.

Though startled, he made the slow journey down
To the stable so cramped and so old.
No longer weary, or wearing a frown,
No longer he felt tired or cold.

A new baby lamb he brought with him there
The youngest with softest of fleece.
Tenderly carried with greatest of care,
A gift for the child Prince of peace.

Leaning down at an opening he entered the stall,
Inside the light shone oh so bright.
Tears filled his eyes, on his knees he did fall
In homage to God on that night.

Both Mary and Joseph knelt by the child
As asleep baby Jesus did nod.
On the night that a shepherd simple and mild,
Brought a lamb to the pure Lamb of God.

****

RESTORING

Like tears from Mother Natures eyes,
The rain came falling,falling.
Quenching the thirst of parched dry earth
For waters calling,calling.

Trickling down through crevice and crack,
Dormant seed beds drinking,drinking.
Causing germination to start
From waters sinking,sinking.

Though desert like, the arid plains
Show signs of greening,greening.
Life now returning blade by blade
With waters preening,preening.

The earth awash with copious draughts
On root shoots pouring,pouring.
Land once bare, now sprouting grass,
Pure waters, growth restoring.

****

THE HOUR GLASS.

Slowly fall the sands of time,
Lifes hour glass ever filling.
Neither tide nor time will stall
As grains of sand keep spilling.
Nature has no favourites
And beauty bows to age.
Regardless of their tenure,
To pauper prince or sage.
We can't retrace our footsteps,
Across the sands of time.
Yet they live in memory,
The absurd and sublime.
Where then is the solution;
In life's constant push and shove?
We find it in the caring and
The sharing of God's love.

****

Rhapsody

Moonlight beamed from a stellar sky,
To spread soft light around.
Two lovers strolled in leafy glade
As soft winds sighed their sound.
Hand in hand both shared the dream,
Together was their aim.
Beneath the stars they vowed their love,
Forever would remain.

The music of a rippling rill
Lent rhythm to loves song.
While feint marshmallow cloudlets,
Danced and pranced along.
The prelude opening gently
'Mid lover's rapturous gaze.
The senses heightening sharply,
Yet still the music plays.

Enveloped in the throes of bliss
That crimson clasp called love.
With sweet rhapsodic harmonies
Orchestrated from above.
As timpani and cymbal crashed
Two hearts became as one.
Though the rhapsody had ended,
A new love had just begun.

~~~~~~~~~~~~~~~~~~~~~~~~~~~~~~

By the Lake

At the close of day by the lake I rest,
Amid the hush of Nature's tone.
Reflected here in its mirrored waters
A solitary stork stands alone.

Now softest murmurs rippling through leaves,
Whisper gently the promise of night.
Where blue of the day enjoins evening glow,
As the stork once again takes to flight.

Layer after layer, darkness takes hold,
Stars slowly invading the sky.
Peace comes in waves falling silently down,
The wind greets it all with a sigh.

Here I find a sanctuary of rest,
To sit and relax for a time.
Nature at evening is dressed in her best,
With a beauty, simply sublime.

~~~~~~~~~~~~~~~~~~~~~~~~~~~~~~~

Dreamer

Pale shafts of moonlight
Caressing your hair.
As nights incantations
Fall soft on the air.
Deeply you're sleeping,
Gently you dream,
Guarded by angels
And starlight agleam.
Safe now you slumber
As peace overflows.
Calmed from all caring
In restful repose.
Cherubs spread stardust
On gossamer wings.
Out in the distance
A nightingale sings,
Sleep on sweet dreamer
Till dawn sends its light.
Bringing a new day
And farewell to night.

Into the Stillness

Somewhere beyond the heart and mind
A journey toward soul.
In stillness softer than a mist;
A yielding of control.

Here dwells silent serenity,
The peace of inner truth.
Where age is not a consequence
Dependent on your youth.

Internal hopes and dreams become
Refreshed, restored, renewed.
Like streams of crystal water;
Should the spirit be confused.

Come sit in contemplation,
Life's purpose to fulfill,
Enlightened through the power of love.
Mid the presence of the still.

~~~~~~~~~~~~~~~~~~~~~~~~~~~~~~

TOMORROWS TASK TODAY

How often do we stop and say,
Let's leave that job for another day.
It will give us some more time for fun,
But will that job be ever done?

The secret is to make a start
Slowly at first no need to dart.
Then bit by bit see progress build
And you begin to feel fulfilled.

Just face your tasks with eager will
You'll find that it's not all uphill.
There's Joy in seeing your job well done,
But you'll never find it, if you haven't begun.

Tides wait for no one and time will not stall
So while it's still early decide on a call.
To that elderly neighbour who lives down your way,
While tomorrow is yours--- he may just have today.

~~~~~~~~~~~~~~~~~~~~~~~~~~~~~~~~~~~~~~

MAUDE AND CLAUDE.
(With apologies to Alfred, Lord Tennyson.)

Come into the garden Maude,
Let us lie among the peas.
In sublimation shall we lay
Mid myriads of fleas.
Soon shall we play Tennys on
The lawn so lush and green.
You on bat and I on ball
A transport so serene.
Here as Woodbines spices waft,
Your senses to beguile.
Come share with me of lovers draft
As we linger for a while.

I'll not come to your garden Claude
For I fear of your intention.
Yet green although your peas may be
Your Fleas defy convention.
As for your Tennys on the lawn
To me it sounds quite wicked.
Should it be played by bat and ball
It's not Tennys Claude. It's cricket.
The spice of your sweet Woodbine
Does nought for one like me.
So I'll not come to your garden Claude,
T'is not where a lass should be

~~~~~~~~~~~~~~~~~~~~~~~~~~~~~~

Lament

Oh come you mists of morning,

Come mists of evening too.

Lay gently on the willow

And I will weep with you.

Be it sunlight,

Be it moonlight

Bring my lost love,

Bring my soul

Bring her amid your foggy dew

While doleful prayer bells toll

~~~~~~~~~~~~~~~~~~~~~~~~~~~

THE SOURCE

My mind was a confusion
And nothing seemed to count.
Friends were an intrusion
And troubles seemed to mount.
Life's journey heading nowhere,
Each step led me off course.
My spirit like an arid stream
Was cut off from its source.

All pathways were uneven,
None narrow or none straight.
I questioned in my heart space
And its answer was "just wait".
A solution to my yearning,
My best efforts failed to force.
How could I know? How could I win?
Without a loving source.

Then one day in my frustration,
I called out in deep despair.
"Oh Lord my will I yield to you,
Please listen to my prayer".
As tears began descending
Caused by sorrow and remorse.
My heart was filled with grace and love
From an overflowing source.

Like streams of living water
That heal the weary and the weak.
This flow of love is there for all,
If only we would seek.
The gift of His salvation
That from Calvary freely pours.
The blood of Jesus Christ my Lord,
My God, my only source.

****

STARSCAPE.

Midwinter revelry fades into mist,
On an evening stroll in the fells.
Beneath a canopy deep and dark blue,
Where peace and contentment indwells.

Along by the lakeside the voices of night,
Sing a nocturnal chorus in tune.
Orion the hunter a sentinel stands,
A wolf howls its cry to the Moon.

Stars in their clusters set heaven ablaze
Planets pulsing amid nature's void.
Like a million grains of luminous sand,
Washed up by a galactic tide.

Be-speckled by tiny pinpoints of light,
Twinkling, blinking in perfect array.
A festoon composed upon the night sky,
God's Jewellery goes on display.

~~~~~~~~~~~~~~~~~~~~~~~~~~~~~~

Tidal Urge

Murmuring wavelets wash on the shore

Eager lovers tenderly entwine

The pulse of the ocean calm and slow

Soft sea breezes and mellow moonshine

Two heartbeats thrum to its tidal song

Passion rises with the waters swell

Love's dream fulfilled in blissful embrace

Where sea and sand and sky cast their spell

****

Life's Threshold

Forever must I stand in faltering fear
To do, to be, to venture, or to stay?
The choice is only mine and mine alone,
To step beyond the problems of each day.

Should I follow a fraternity of fools
And fade into tomorrow's emptiness.
Or bravely grasp the nettle named "Today"
To claim its hidden height of happiness?

Whatever fate or fortune has in store.
However destiny may deal her hand.
Though influence or circumstance deride,
Uncertain, on life's threshold here I stand.

~~~~~~~~~~~~~~~~~~~~~~~~~~~

Ode to a Duck

She came into our house one day,
From where we'll never know.
But looks as though she's here to stay,
She doesn't want to go.
She paddles in the puddles,
She paddles in the muck,
She paddles in our wading pond,
She's just a paddling duck.
She paddles in the kitchen
And paddles on the floor.
Then when she sees the bathroom,
She paddles all the more.
She's grown quite fond of granddad,
Coz she paddles on his bed
And as he tries to have a snooze,
She paddles on his head.
Now if you've lost a paddling duck,
If you're sad and feeling pain,
Just call around to our house,
You can have her back again.

~~~~~~~~~~~~~~~~~~~~~~~~~~~~

FADED DREAMS

Dreams that once were mine to own,
Promised life and love to me.
I dared to take them, not on loan
But for all eternity.

Crystal clear, ambitions plan,
The road map all planned out.
A boy soon to become a man,
Of my dreams, I had no doubt.

Dreams along careers path guiding,
Efforts tailored to the chore.
Soon outside the dream providing,
The wherewithal for life and more.

Heart and home my dreams bestowed.
Family now part of the scheme.
Blessings and comfort overflowed,
In a seeming never ending stream.

Filled with awe and puerile wonder,
I to dreamers could relate.
Yet ones dreams can fall asunder,
Fallen victims of cruel fate.

Soon the lords of econ' trading,
Signified financial crash.
My dream of success, now fading.
Hopes, ambitions, gone in a flash.

Even love's bright light is dying
And life is not what it seems.
Thoughts of future petrifying,
As I live with faded dreams.

****

Orchestration

Stars arranged across
The firmament,
Like grains of sand
Randomly cast
And suspended upon
The heavens.
Faithful and constant
in their place.
Beating with
The rhythmic pulse
Of God's orchestra.
Dense the darkest,
Backdrop lain to
Emphasize dimension.
A full moon, the
silver spotlight,
As Sagittarius and
Andromeda perform
A galactic dance,
With the silky
milky way.
Seated on a
Heavenly throne,
The Orchestrator
Heaves a contented sigh.

****

Placid Waters

Upon a morning bright and clear,
By a placid lake I strolled.
In reeds along its lapping shore,
Hid the bright marsh marigold.

The surface, mirrored clearest blue
Reflecting heavenly sky.
With swallows swooping all around,
Clouds were floating gently by.

Eerie and plaintive came a cry;
The lonely call of a loon.
An answer echoed back again,
From across the wide lagoon.

Birds chirping out their mating song,
Filled the air with joyous sound.
A tender breeze caressed the trees,
Where the cherry buds are found.

With Spring awakening everywhere;
Nature's treasure to extol.
Her gift of natural beauty,
Was a balm to heart and soul.

~~~~~~~~~~~~~~~~~~~~~~~~~

REPOSE

Away from trouble's tumult,
A respite I propose.
Wandering in fantasy,
Through sweet, serene repose.

Where mountains, sea and lakeside,
Are salves to ease our pain
And skies of blue, appearing through
The grey clouds filled with rain.

Deeper into slumbers shade,
A transport to on high.
Eagles soaring, wild and free.
Our spirits with them fly.

By placid pools restoring,
All tensions dissipate.
Softened by tranquility,
In dreamlike, restful state.

Relaxed, at one with nature,
Her peace now overflows.
Comfort from the cares of day,
We find in calm repose.

****

Orpheus in his Underwear

Orpheus, oh Orpheus
Your dancing is preposterous
Attired in just your underwear
Doing the Can-Can on a chair

Were Offenbach alive today
He'd turn in his grave I have to say
So before the band begins to play
Put on your trousers…Orpheus

Eurydice is overcome
By the overhang of your fat bum
'Ere the timpanist should roll the drum
Put on your trousers…..Orpheus

~~~~~~~~~~~~~~~~~~~~~~~~~

Mistified!

Gently drifting evening mist
Moves slowly in from sea.
Shading all the land around
Across the hills and lea.
Hazy moonshine from on high
Creates a spectral glow.
Adding mystery to the night
Upon the ground below..

Calm and still the night time air,
No rustles from the leaves.
Silence saturates the scene,
No whispering in the eaves.
Evening dew bedecks the lawn
Reflecting moonlights glow.
Mist is slowly lifting as...
A light breeze starts to blow..

Lonely comes the hooting cry
From distant barnyard Owl.
Re-echoed by the moonsong
Of a wild wolfs' wailing howl..
Welcoming the light on high
Across that great divide.
No longer dimly fogbound
No longer mystified.

~~~~~~~~~~~~~~~~~~~~

The Masters Voice

In the rippling of the river
And the whispering of the breeze.
In the distant peal of thunder
And the droning of the bees.

In the surf's wash on the seashore
And the blackbird's evening tune.
In the pattering of raindrops
And the owl's cry to the moon.

In the laughter of a baby
And the squeal of gulls on high.
In the soothing calm of music
And the sound of lover's sigh.

In the quietude of night time
And the sun filled skies of blue.
In His symphony of nature,
The master speaks to you

****

Golden Epilogue.

A cobbled roadway, leads onto the garden
That sits beyond the lamplights gentle glow
Hazy mists, are drifting like a spectre
Or phantom ships which softly come and go

A sleepy blackbird sings the days surrender
With sweetly fluted, languid, evening song
As darkness draws her mantle o'er the lily-pond
An orchestra of crickets sing along.

Leaves of yellowed green lie loosely scattered,
While crimson, gold and brown still bravely stall.
An erratic westerly wind disturbs them;
As confetti like, they begin to fall.

Slight ripples on the pond reflect the moonshine,
Of a lonely hunters moon on her rise.
Dancing with a shimmer through the water.
To background of the wind's seductive sighs.

Oh Nature shall I ever hold such beauty,
As your Autumn's dappled colors all aglow.
Alas I fear that miracle shall pass me
When Winter fills the plains with rain and snow.

****

Notes

Notes